Contents

What you need (eq

1 Estimating

2 Graphs   19

3 Formulas   32

4 Scale drawing   41

5 Volume   50

6 Speed   68

7 Views   86

CW01066628

What you need

Page 5   Worksheet BT-1

Page 15   Worksheet BT-2

Pages 19–31   2 mm graph paper

Page 42   Square spotty paper

Page 46   Worksheet BT-3
                  Graph paper, scissors, ruler marked in mm

Page 76   Dice

Page 81   Graph paper

Page 89   Worksheet BT-4
                  Scissors, glue

Page 92   Worksheet BT-5
                  3 ordinary matchboxes

Published by the Press Syndicate of the University of Cambridge
The Pitt Building, Trumpington Street, Cambridge CB2 1RP
32 East 57th Street, New York, NY 10022, USA
10 Stamford Road, Oakleigh, Melbourne 3166, Australia

© Cambridge University Press 1985

First published 1985
Third printing 1987

Printed in Great Britain at the University Press, Cambridge

ISBN 0 521 31665 0

Illustrations by Chris Evans and David Parkins

Photographs by Tim Thomas

The authors and the publisher would like to thank P. J. Robinson/Colourviews Ltd
for permission to reproduce the copyright photograph on page 75.

Estimating

Estimating heights and lengths

Estimating means having a good guess at the size of something.

A1 (a) Guess how long your pen or pencil is, in centimetres.
         Write down your estimate.

    (b) Measure the length and see how close you were.

A2 (a) Estimate the height of your classroom door, in metres.
         Write down your estimate.

    (b) Find out the real height. See how close you were.

A3 Estimate these in **centimetres.**

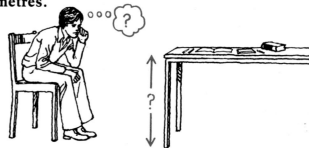

(a) The height of your table or desk from the ground

(b) The height of your chair seat from the ground

(c) The length and width of your desk or table

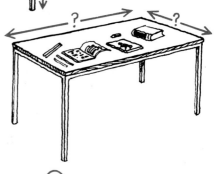

(d) The lengths of the sides of this page of the book

Now check all your estimates by measuring.

Estimating by stepping off

This drawing shows a man climbing a telegraph pole.

The man is about 2 m tall.
We can use this to estimate the height of the pole.

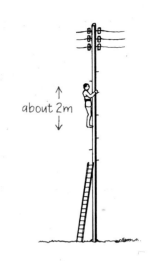

about 2m

1 First we make two marks on the edge of a piece of paper, like this.

2 Then we see how many times we can 'step off' this length along the pole.

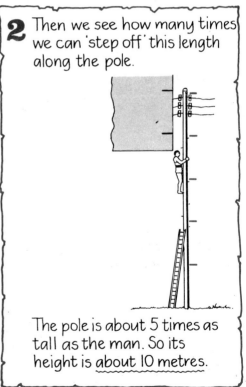

The pole is about 5 times as tall as the man. So its height is about 10 metres.

1   You need worksheet BT-1.

This is a drawing
of a goldfish.

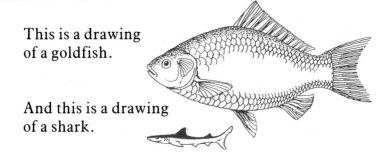

And this is a drawing
of a shark.

You cannot compare the lengths of the two fish by 'stepping off'.
This is because the two fish are drawn to **different scales**.

The goldfish is drawn about $\frac{1}{2}$ of its full size.
The shark is drawn about $\frac{1}{100}$ of its full size.

You can only compare lengths by 'stepping off' when objects
are drawn to the **same scale**.

The 'thumb and pencil' method of stepping off

These two snakes are drawn to the same scale.

You can compare their lengths without marking the
drawings, like this.

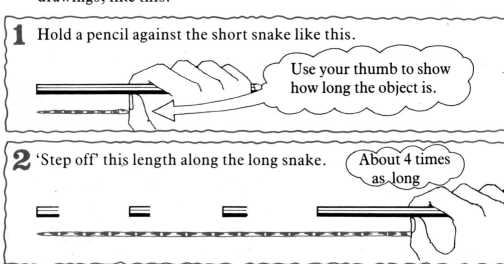

1 Hold a pencil against the short snake like this.

Use your thumb to show
how long the object is.

2 'Step off' this length along the long snake.

About 4 times
as long

2 During the Second World War, people thought
   the Lancaster bomber was a very big plane.

   See how the Lancaster compares with some present-day planes,
   and with a bus.

   The bus is 10 metres long.
   Estimate the length of each plane, in metres.

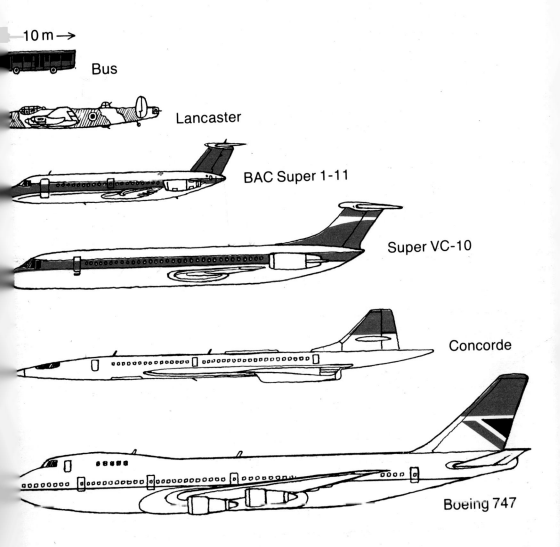

—10 m →

Bus

Lancaster

BAC Super 1-11

Super VC-10

Concorde

Boeing 747

B3 This picture shows some swords and daggers laid out in a museum.

Dagger A is about 15 cm long. Estimate the length of each of the other daggers and swords.

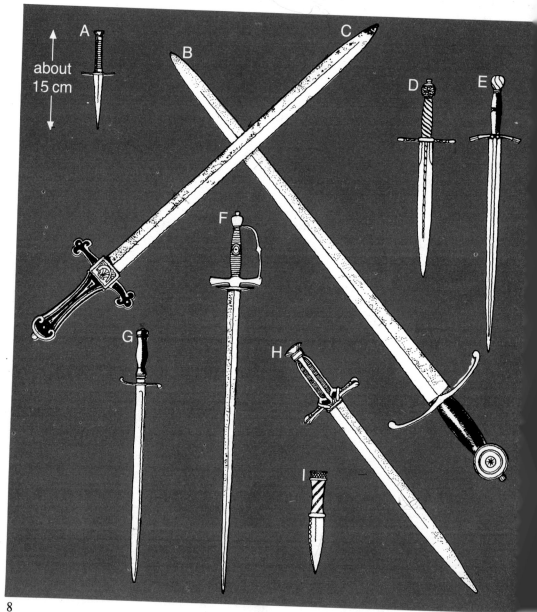

C Estimating a short length from a long one

1 These two needles are drawn to the same scale.
Check that the long one is about 5 times as long
as the short one.

The long needle is about 30 cm long.
How long is the short one, roughly?

2 These two bolts are drawn to the same scale.

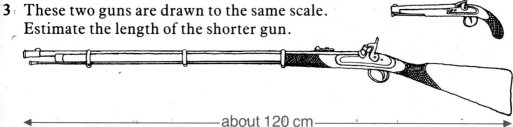

←————————— about 20 cm —————————→

The long bolt is about 20 cm long.
Estimate the length of the short bolt. (First find out roughly
how many times the short length goes into the long one.)

3 These two guns are drawn to the same scale.
Estimate the length of the shorter gun.

←————————— about 120 cm —————————→

4 This glove and this scarf are drawn to the same scale.
Estimate the length of the glove.

←——————— about 150 cm ———————→

C5 This is a view looking down on a harbour.
The large ship is about 200 m long.

Estimate the length of each of the smaller ships.

More than half or less than half?

1 A Mini is 11 feet long.
A Rolls-Royce is 20 feet long.

   (a) Is the Mini **more** than half, or **less** than half as long
as the Rolls-Royce?

   (b) Which of these two scale drawings shows the cars correctly?

A    B

2 Mrs Worthington's height is
about 160 cm.
Her daughter Sarah's height
is about 70 cm.

Which of these two scale drawings
shows them correctly?

(**Think**. Is Sarah's height
more, or less, than half her
mother's height?)

A   B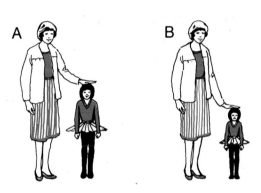

3 A tree is 22 m tall and a lamp post is 9 m tall.
Which of these scale drawings is correct?

A

B

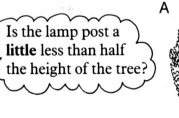
Is the lamp post a
little less than half
the height of the tree?

Or is it **much** less
than half the height
of the tree?

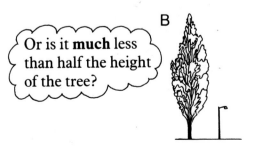

D4 A liner, 160 m long, is alongside a tanker, 300 m long.
▲ Which scale drawing shows them correctly?

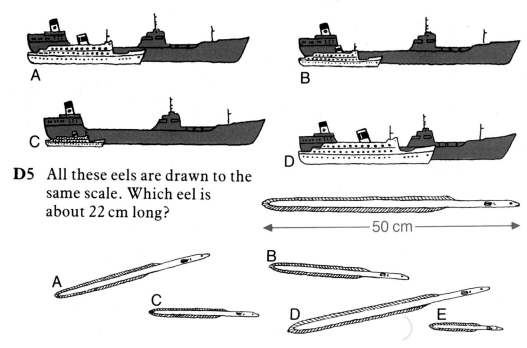

A   B

C   D

D5 All these eels are drawn to the same scale. Which eel is about 22 cm long?

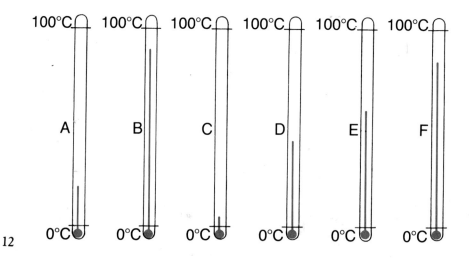

— 50 cm —

A   B   C   D   E

D6 (a) Which of these thermometers shows a temperature of 60 °C?
    (b) Which shows a temperature of 21 °C?

100°C	100°C	100°C	100°C	100°C	100°C
A	B	C	D	E	F
0°C	0°C	0°C	0°C	0°C	0°C

12

7 This beaker holds 500 ml when it is full.

Which of these drawings shows the same beaker with 275 ml of liquid in it?

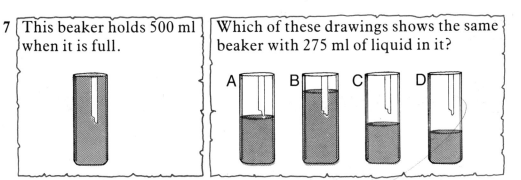

A   B   C   D

8 The tallest man of all time was 267 cm tall.
The shortest male adult dwarf was 67 cm tall.
Which of these scale drawings shows them correctly?

A   B   C

9 Blagdon Football Club's pitch is 120 m long and 54 m wide.
Which of these is the plan of the pitch?

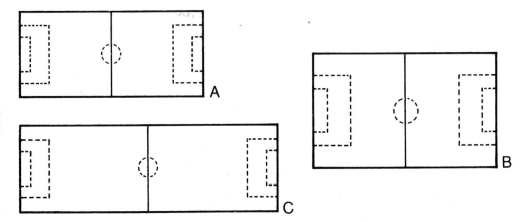

A   B   C

E Halving and quartering

E1 Halving a line by eye

1 Draw a straight line.

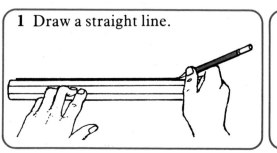

2 Do not use your ruler.
Estimate where
the half-way point is.
Mark it on your line.

3 Now measure each part of your line.
If your estimate was good,
the two parts should be roughly equal.

4 Draw three more lines and
do the same. (Try it with
quite a long line!)

This is how you can mark the **quarter points** of a line.

1 First mark the half-way point.

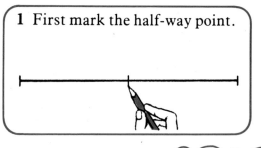

2 Then mark the half-way point
of each half.

This point is
$\frac{1}{4}$ of the way along.

This point is
$\frac{3}{4}$ of the way along.

E2 Draw a straight line.
Estimate where to mark the quarter points.
Then measure each part of the line.
Check that the four parts are roughly equal.
Draw two more lines and do the same.

You can use halving and quartering to help you estimate heights and lengths in scale drawings.

This scale drawing shows a tribesman and his son. The tribesman is about 200 cm tall.

You can estimate the son's height, like this.

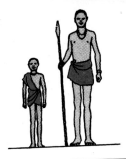

1 Put the edge of a piece of paper against the drawing of the tribesman.
Mark his height on the paper.

2 Divide the height into halves and quarters. Estimate where to put the marks.

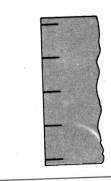

3 The tribesman is about 200 cm tall. $\frac{1}{4}$ of this is 50 cm. Label your scale.

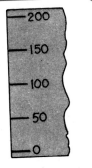

4 Use your scale to estimate the son's height.

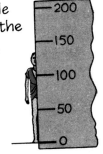

It is between 100cm and 150 cm, but nearer to 150 cm. A rough estimate is about 130 cm.

3 You need worksheet BT-2.

E4 This is a scale drawing of
the tower of Liverpool Cathedral.
The tower's height is 100 m.

Estimate the heights of A and B.

E5 This is a scale drawing o
Nelson's Column.

Estimate the heights of
C and D.

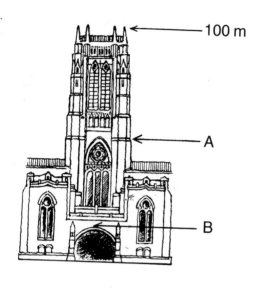

100 m

A

B

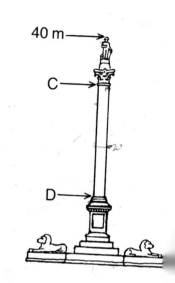

40 m

C

D

E6 This is a scale drawing of Durham Cathedral.
Estimate the heights of E and F.

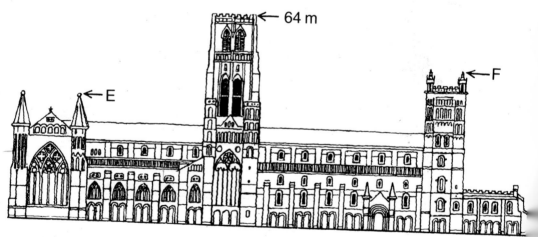

64 m

E

F

7 This is a scale drawing of the Eiffel Tower.

Estimate the heights of A and B.

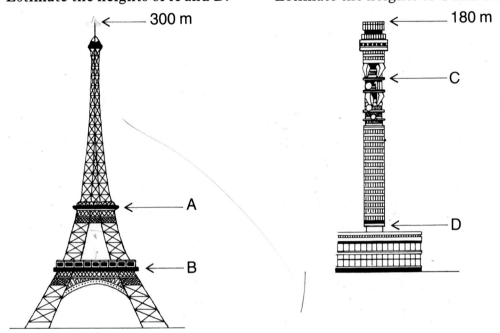

E8 This is a scale drawing of the Post Office tower.

Estimate the heights of C and D.

9 Estimate the temperature which each of these thermometers shows.

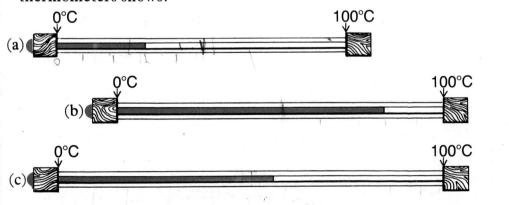

E10 There are two church towers in this picture, A and B.

2 Graphs

A The axes of a graph

This graph shows the temperature inside an oven after it was switched on.

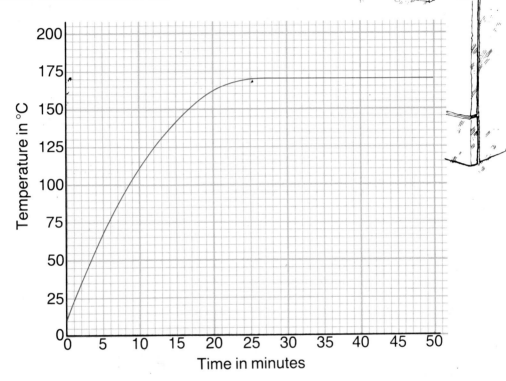

Each scale on a graph is called an **axis**.
On this graph the two **axes** (ax-eez) show time in minutes and temperature in °C.

Going **across**, each small square stands for 1 minute.
But going **up**, each small square stands for **5 degrees**.

A1 (a) What was the temperature of the oven at the start?
▲ (b) What was the highest temperature it reached?
(c) How long did it take to reach its highest temperature?

The graphs on this page and the next were made by two different temperature recording machines.

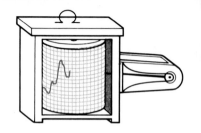

A2

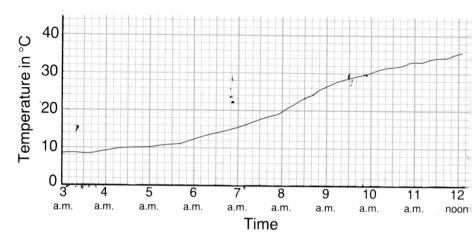

(a) Look at the temperature axis on this graph.
How many degrees does each small square stand for?

(b) Look at the time axis.
There are 6 small squares between 3 a.m. and 4 a.m.
How many minutes does each small square stand for?

(c) Find 8:40 a.m. on the time axis.
What was the temperature at 8:40 a.m.? (**Not** 22 °C!)

(d) What was the temperature at 9:30 a.m.?

(e) What was it at 7:10 a.m.?

(f) Find 30 °C on the temperature axis.
Follow the line across from 30 °C until you get to the graph.

At what time was the temperature 30°C?

3

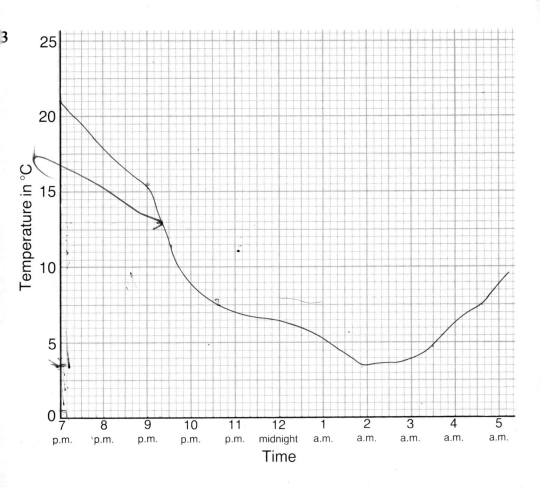

(a) What does 1 small square on the temperature axis of this graph stand for?

(b) What was the temperature at 9 p.m.?

(c) What was it at 3:30 a.m.?

(d) What was the lowest temperature recorded on the graph?

(e) At what time was the temperature 13°C?

(f) There were two times when the temperature was 5·5°C. What times were they?

B Plotting a graph

A science teacher put
a dish of hot water
next to an open window.

Various pupils took
the temperature of the water
during the next few minutes.

It was 83 °C at the start.

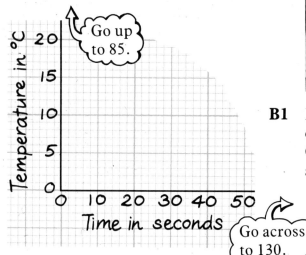

B1 Draw axes like these
on graph paper.
Go across as far as 130 seconds
and up as far as 85 °C.

Here are Daniel's readings.

Time after start, in seconds	0	50	80	90	130
Temperature, in °C	83	41	26	23	14

Mark the five points on your graph.
We call this **plotting** the points.
Do not join the points up.

2 Look at the five points you have plotted.
Guess what the temperature might have been
60 seconds after the start.
Write down your guess. Do **not** mark it on the graph.

3 Here are Jane's readings.
Plot them on the **same graph** as Daniel's.

Time after start, in seconds	0	20	60	120
Temperature, in °C	83	65	35	16

4 Guess the temperature 30 seconds from the start.
Write down your guess. Do **not** plot it.

5 These are David's readings. Plot them on the same graph.

Time after start, in seconds	0	10	40	70	110
Temperature, in °C	83	76	48	30	18

6 Sandra's readings come next.
She made a mistake when she wrote down
one of the temperatures.

Time after start, in seconds	0	30	35	65	100	125
Temperature, in °C	83	56	57	33	20	14·5

(a) Plot Sandra's points.

(b) Put a ring round the point you think is wrong.
Put a point in where you think it should be.

So far your graph looks something like this.

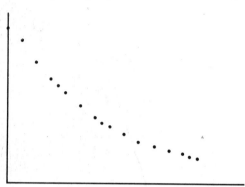

B7 Toby took the temperature of the water at 5, 15, 45, 55 and 115 seconds after the start.

Put in points where you think his readings would be.

B8 Suppose more children in the class had taken readings.

Guess where the extra points could be and put them on your graph.

Heating water

David heated some water.
He took its temperature
from time to time.

At the start, the temperature
was 11 °C.

Here are David's readings.

Time in seconds	0	20	40	60	80	100	120
Temperature in °C	11	30	45	58	68	75	80

1 Draw axes going
across to 120
and up to 80.
Start the axes like this.

Plot the seven points
from the table.

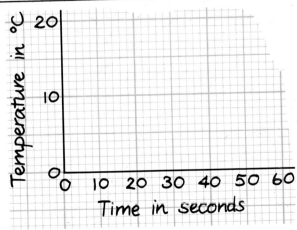

Your graph should look something like this.

All you have is seven points.

You do not know what the temperature was in between these seven points.

But it is most likely that the temperature went up gradually all the time.

So the complete graph would be a smooth curve, like this.

This is the sort of graph you would get from a temperature recorder.

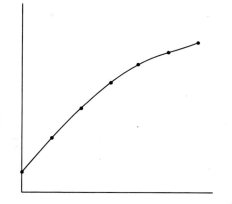

C2 (a) Draw a smooth curve through the points you plotted.

   (b) What do you think the temperature was 50 seconds after the start?

C3 Rhonda heated some water and took these readings.

Time in seconds	0	10	20	30	40	50	60
Temperature in °C	6	16	22	26	29	31	32

Draw axes, plot the points and draw a smooth curve through them.

Touch down

An aircraft is coming in to land.
The co-pilot notes the speed of the
aircraft every 5 seconds.

Here are the readings.

Time in seconds	0	5	10	15	20	25	30
Speed in m.p.h.	150	150	140	120	90	80	80

Time in seconds	35	40	45	50	55	60
Speed in m.p.h.	70	60	40	10	5	5

1 (a) Draw axes like these.

Plot the points and
draw a smooth curve
through them.

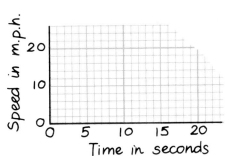

(b) There are four stages in making the landing.

(1) First the pilot reduces speed to 80 m.p.h.

(2) Then he or she keeps the aircraft at
this speed while touching down on
the runway.

(3) Then the speed is reduced again while
the aircraft is on the runway.

(4) Finally the aircraft moves slowly off
the runway.

Label your graph as shown here.

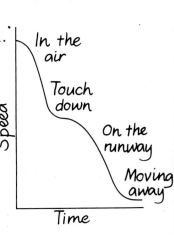

27

E High tide

This table shows the depth of the water in a harbour
at various times in the afternoon.

Time	2 p.m.	3 p.m.	4 p.m.	5 p.m.	6 p.m.	7 p.m.	8 p.m
Depth in metres	1·3	2·3	3·2	3·9	4·1	3·8	3·0

E1 (a) Draw axes like these.

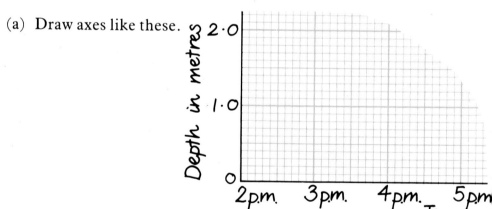

(b) What does 1 small square stand for on the 'depth' axis?

(c) Plot the points from the table.
Draw a smooth curve through them.

(d) From your graph find the depth of the water at 4:30 p.m.

(e) Find the depth of the water at 3:45 p.m.

F Marking axes

Sophie planted a sunflower seed.
When the plant started to grow, she measured
its height.
She measured it again after 1 week, 2 weeks, 3 weeks.

Here are the measurements.

Time in weeks	0	1	2	3
Height in cm	1	4	6	8

Then Sophie went on holiday.
She could not measure the plant at 4 weeks or 5 weeks.
The next measurements she made were at 6 weeks and 7 weeks.

Here is the complete table.

Time in weeks	0	1	2	3	6	7
Height in cm	1	4	6	8	15	17

Sophie drew these axes and
plotted the points from her
table.

**But she has done something
wrong already.**

What has she done wrong?

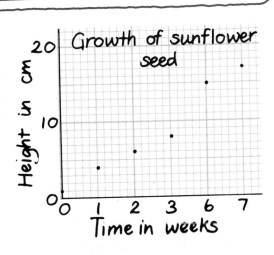

29

Sophie's graph is wrong because **the time axis is not numbered in equal steps.**

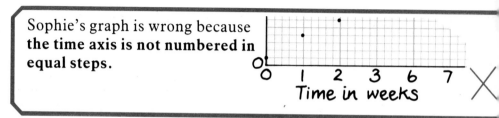

The time axis should be marked as shown here.

When the points are plotted, you can see the gap where Sophie went on holiday.

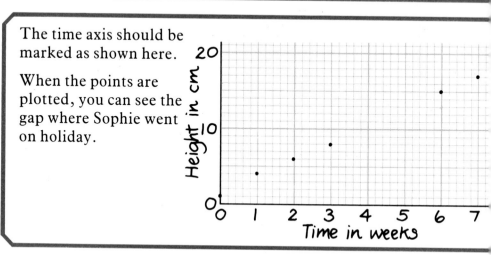

F2 Hema took her baby to the clinic every now and then and had it weighed.

Here is the baby's weight record.

Age in months	0	1	2	4	6	7	9
Weight in kg	4·0	5·0	6·5	7·5	8·5	9·0	9·5

Draw a graph of the baby's weight. Start the axes as shown on the right.

Draw a smooth curve through the points.

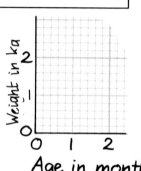

3 Colin lit a candle. Every now and then he measured its height.

Here are his measurements.

Time in hours since candle was lit	0	1	2	3	5	6	7	9	11
Height in cm	29	23	19	16	12	10	8·5	5·5	3

Draw a graph of the candle's height.
Start the axes as shown on the right.

Draw a smooth curve through the points.

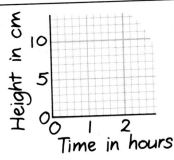

F4 A boy drew this graph to show how Britain's railways grew between 1833 and 1851.

What is wrong with the graph?

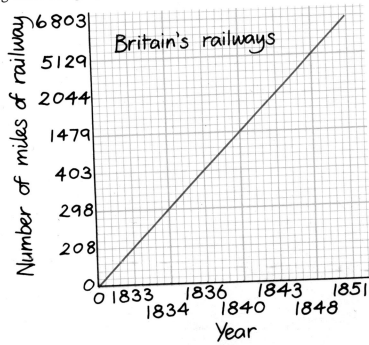

3 Formulas

A Doorsteps

Jim is a builder.

He makes doorsteps with red and white tiles.

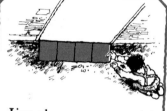

Jim always starts with a row of red tiles.

Then he puts a row of white tiles against the red tiles.

Then he puts 2 white tiles at each end to finish the doorstep.

A1 How many white tiles will Jim use if he starts with a row of 8 red tiles?

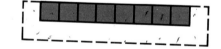

A2 How many white tiles will he use if he starts with
(a) 5 red tiles   (b) 9 red tiles

A3 Write your answers to questions A1 and A2 in a table, like this.

Leave room in the table for some more numbers.

Number of red tiles	Number of white tiles
8 →	...
5 →	...
9 →	...

A4

Jim starts with 40 red tiles.

He puts a row of white tiles against them.

Then he adds the white tiles at each end. How many white tiles does he use altogether?

Write in your table
40 ⟶ ...

A5   Jim starts with 100 red tiles.

How many white tiles does he need?

Write in the table   100 ⟶ ...

A6   When you know the number of red tiles you can work out the number of white tiles.

Write down the rule you use.

The rule in question A6 is this:

> Start with the **number of red tiles.** Add on 4. What you get is equal to the **number of white tiles.**

There is a short way to write this rule.
We let r stand for the **number of red tiles,**
and w stand for the **number of white tiles.**

We write the rule like this: $r + 4 = w$. This is called a **formula.**

A7 Work out w when r is   (a) 17   (b) 29   (c) 95   (d) 106

B   Chain fences

These are drawings of chain fences.
The first fence has 5 posts and 4 chains.

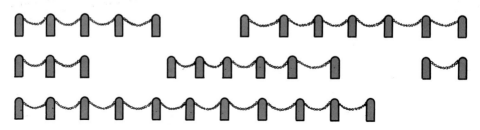

B1 Count the number of posts and the number of chains in each fence.

p	c
5	→ 4

Make a table like the one shown here, and write the numbers in it. (p stands for the number of posts, and c stands for the number of chains.)

B2   When you know p, there is a rule for working out c.
▲   Write the rule as a formula.

34

Horses

1 (a) Count the legs of the horses in this picture.

   (b) How many horses are there?

2 Copy and complete this table.

Number of legs	Number of horses
12	→
4	→
8	→
36	→
20	→

3 Let l stand for the number of legs.
   ▲ Let h stand for the number of horses.

   When you know l, there is a rule for working out h.
   Write the rule as a formula.

4 (a) If $l = 40$, what is h?

   (b) If $l = 24$, what is h?

C5 Each van holds 3 horses.

How many horses will 5 vans hold?

C6 Copy and complete this table.

Number of vans	Number of horses
5 ⟶	
2 ⟶	
8 ⟶	
10 ⟶	
100 ⟶	

C7 Let v stand for the number of vans.
Let h stand for the number of horses.

When you know v there is a formula for working out h.

Write the formula.

C8 (a) If $v = 7$, what is h?

(b) If $v = 20$, what is h?

C9 (Careful!) If h is 18, what is v?

D   Cars and motorbikes

Gold is being carried to the bank.
Each armoured car has a motorbike on each side,
and there is one motorbike in front and one at the back.

D1 There are 4 cars in the picture. How many motorbikes are there?

D2 If there are 7 cars, how many motorbikes do they need?

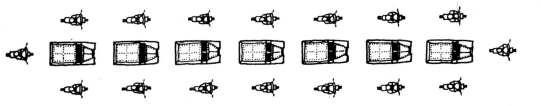

D3 (a) How many motorbikes do they need for 20 cars?

(b) How can you **work out** the number of motorbikes
without drawing a picture or counting?

(c) Work out the number of motorbikes needed for 100 cars.

When you know the number of cars, you can work out
the number of motorbikes, like this:

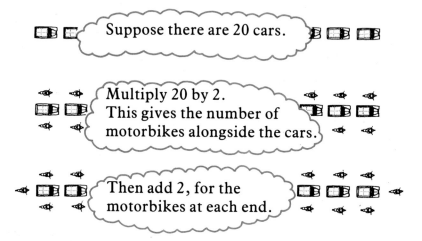

Suppose there are 20 cars.

Multiply 20 by 2.
This gives the number of
motorbikes alongside the cars.

Then add 2, for the
motorbikes at each end.

Let *c* stand for the number of cars,
and *m* for the number of motorbikes.

The rule for working out *m* can be written as a formula:

$$(c \times 2) + 2 = m$$

Notice the **brackets**. They tell us to multiply *c* by 2 **first,**
before adding 2.

Using the formula

Suppose we want to know *m* when *c* is 10.
We replace *c* in the formula by 10.

$$
\begin{aligned}
(c \times 2) + 2 &= m \\
(10 \times 2) + 2 &= m \\
20 \quad + 2 &= m \\
22 &= m
\end{aligned}
$$

So *m* is 22.

D4 If *c* is 8, what is *m*? Set out the working as above.

E   Using formulas

E1   This scaffolding tower is made from metal tubes, each 1 metre long.

(a)   Count the number of 1-metre tubes in the tower.

(b)   There is a formula for calculating the number of tubes. It is

$$(h \times 8) + 4 = t.$$

h is the height of the tower in metres.
t is the number of tubes.

Use this formula to find the number of tubes in the tower in the picture, showing your working.

Check that the answer agrees with your answer to (a).

(c)   Use the formula to find the number of tubes in a tower of height

(i) 4 metres   (ii) 7 metres   (iii) 10 metres

(d)   Jan has 100 1-metre tubes. Does she have enough to make a tower 12 metres high? If not, how many more does she need?

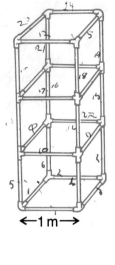

←1 m→

E2   The formula for a triangular tower like the one shown here is

$$(h \times 6) + 3 = t.$$

Calculate the number of tubes in a triangular tower of height

(a) 3 metres   (b) 8 metres   (c) 20 metres

39

E3 A do-it-yourself shop hires out power tools.

They use this formula to work out the cost of hiring a floor polisher:

$$(d \times 4) + 3 = c.$$

d stands for the number of days for which the polisher is hired. c stands for the cost in pounds.

(a) Work out c when d is   (i) 2   (ii) 5   (iii) 10

(b) Find the cost of hiring the polisher for 8 days.

E4 The same shop uses this formula for working out the cost of hiring a paint sprayer.

$$(d \times 5) + 2 = c$$

(a) Work out c when d is   (i) 3   (ii) 8   (iii) 20

(b) Find the cost of hiring the paint sprayer for 12 days.

E5 You can tell how far away a thunderstorm is by counting seconds. You start counting when you see the lightning, and stop when you hear the thunder.

Then you use the formula $m = s \div 5$.

m stands for the number of miles, and s for the number of seconds.

(a) Calculate m when s is   (i) 20   (ii) 30   (iii) 100

(b) How far away is a thunderstorm if there is a 15-second gap between seeing the lightning and hearing the thunder?

E6 To find the daily amount of food an elephant needs, you divide its weight by 50.

Write this rule as a formula. Use w for the elephant's weight and f for the daily amount of food.

4 Scale drawing

Drawing to scale

Dawn wants to make a wooden nesting box for birds.

The nesting box is made in six pieces.

Dawn has a rectangular piece of wood to cut the pieces from.

Dawn is not sure if her piece of wood is big enough.

This is how she finds out.

She makes a drawing of her piece of wood.
She does not draw it full-size.
She uses 1 cm to stand for 5 cm.

The length of the drawing is 11 cm.
The real piece of wood is 5 times as long as this.
So the real piece of wood is 55 cm long.

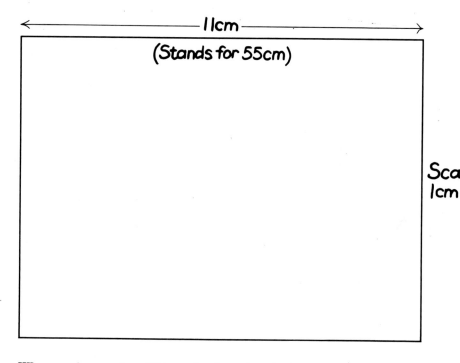

We say the **scale** of Dawn's drawing is **1 cm to 5 cm**.

A1 Measure the short side of the scale drawing.
How long is the short side of the **real** piece of wood?

A2 Copy the scale drawing on square spotty paper.

Now Dawn makes drawings of the six parts of the nesting box.

She draws them to the same scale as before, **1 cm to 5 cm.**

Measure her drawings.
Copy them exactly on spotty paper.

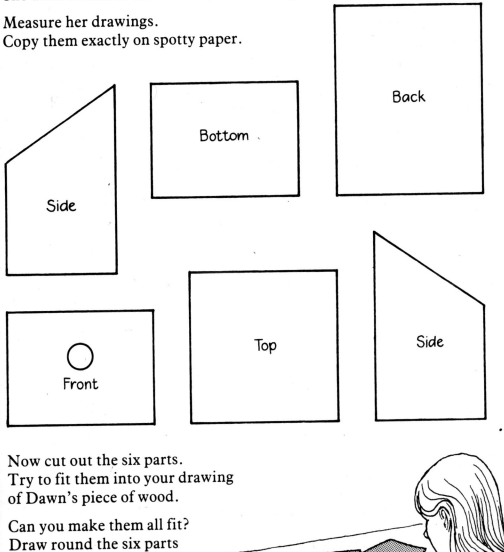

Side

Bottom

Back

Front

Top

Side

Now cut out the six parts.
Try to fit them into your drawing
of Dawn's piece of wood.

Can you make them all fit?
Draw round the six parts
to show where they go.

B Room plans

Dawn shares a room with her sister Kathy.

The plan of the room is opposite.
The scale of the plan is 1 cm to 20 cm.
Each small square stands for a square 10 cm by 10 cm.

B1 (a) What piece of furniture does rectangle A stand for?

(b) Bed B is Dawn's bed. What is its real width in centimetres?

(c) How long is Dawn's bed?

(d) How long is Kathy's bed?

(e) How wide is the gap between the beds?

(f) What does the line C stand for?

(g) What does the dotted curve show?

(h) If you go into the room, is Dawn's bed on your left or your right?

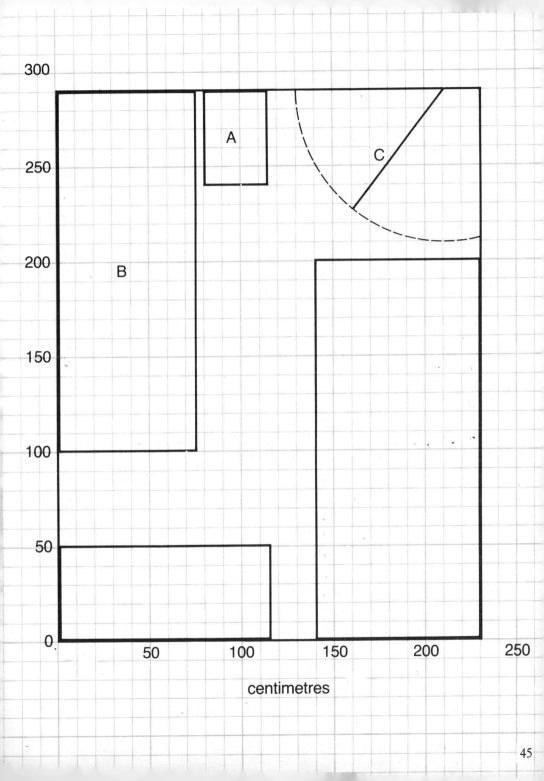

centimetres

You need worksheet BT-3, graph paper, scissors,
a ruler marked in millimetres, like this.

Dawn's family move into
a new house. Now Dawn has
her own bedroom. She wonders
if there will be room for all
her things.

She has a plan of the empty
bedroom. It is on the worksheet.
Each **millimetre** on the plan
stands for **1 centimetre**.

B2 (a) Measure the length of the plan of the room,
in millimetres.

(b) Each millimetre stands for 1 centimetre.
So how long is the real room, in centimetres?

(c) How wide is the real door?

B3 Here is Dawn's chest of drawers.

Can she fit it along the
wall between A and B?

Measure the plan to
find out.

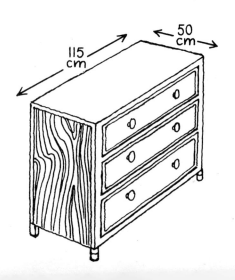

A Model buildings

Sarah is a student at a polytechnic.
She is studying to be an architect (a person
who designs buildings). She has invented
a new method of building, which she calls
CUBUILD ('cube-build').

One of her designs is shown opposite.
The whole building is made up of cubes,
each the same size.

Some cubes are parts of rooms.
Some are parts of staircases or lift shafts.

The drawing below shows one floor of the building.

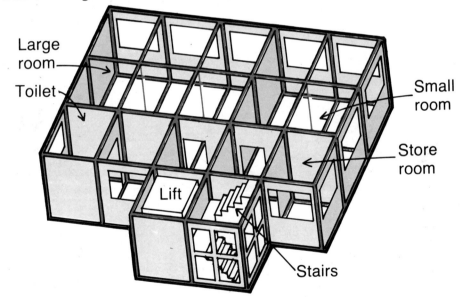

A1 How many cubes are there in this floor?

A2 The building has 4 floors.
How many cubes are there in the whole building?

Models of CUBUILD designs can be
made with centimetre cubes.

Here is a model of the building
you have already seen.

This is how the model
would be constructed.

1 The **ground plan** of the
building is made up of
17 squares, like this.

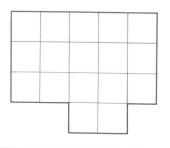

2 The first layer is built
over the ground plan.

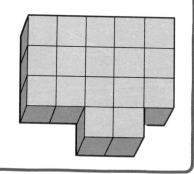

3 Now the second
layer is added . . .

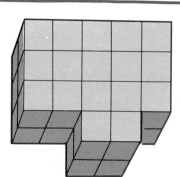

. . . and so on
until there are
4 layers.

3   This is the ground plan
of a CUBUILD building.

The building has 5 layers
of cubes.

(a) How many cubes are there
in each layer?

(b) How many are there in
the whole building?

5 layers

4   How many cubes are there in each of these buildings?

(a)

Ground plan

(6 layers)

(b)

Ground
plan

(3 layers)

(c)

Ground
plan

(10 layers)

(d)

Ground
plan

(7 layers)

53

All the models in this chapter are made with centimetre cubes.

A5 (a) How many square centimetres are there in the ground plan of this model?

(b) How many centimetre cubes are there in the model?

A6 Work out the number of centimetre cubes in each of these models.

(a)

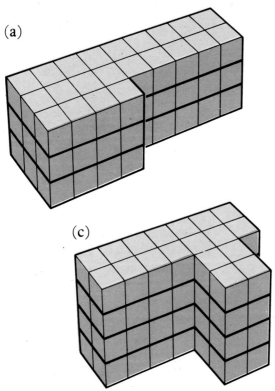

(b)

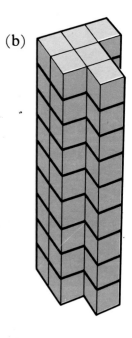

(c)

These two models can each be made
with 8 centimetre cubes.

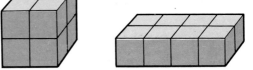

We say the models have the same **volume**.
The volume of a centimetre cube is called **1 cubic cm**.
So the volume of each model is **8 cubic cm**.

7   What are the volumes of these models
in cubic cm?

(a)   (b)   (c)

(d)

(e)

(f)

(g)

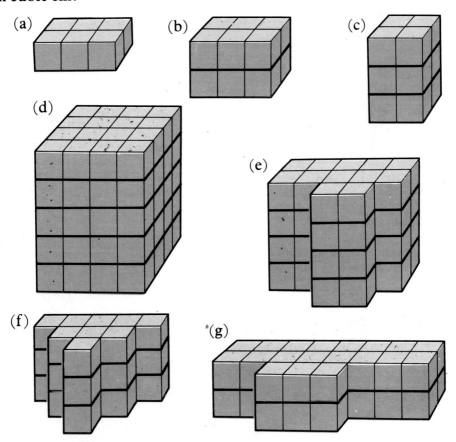

A8 This model has a hole through it, from top to bottom.

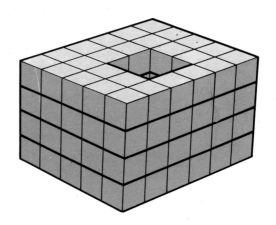

The ground plan looks like this.

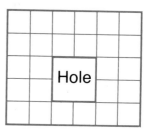

(a) How many squares does the ground plan cover? (Do not count the hole.)

(b) What is the volume of one layer of the model, in cubic cm?

(c) What is the volume of the model?

(d) What is the volume of the hole?

(e) What would the volume of the model be if the hole were filled in?

A9 (a) What is the volume of the hole in this model?

(b) What is the volume of the model?

(c) What would the volume be if the hole were filled in?

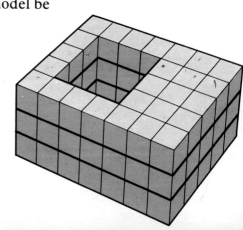

56

B Finding volumes

Up to now, each model has been built
in layers, going upwards.

The layers in this building
are side by side.

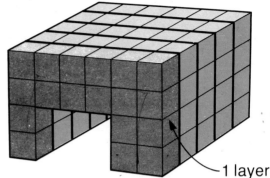

1 layer

B1 (a) How many cubes are there in 1 layer
of the model above?

(b) How many layers are there?

(c) How many cubes are there in the whole model?

B2 What is the volume, in cubic centimetres,
of each of these models?

(a)

(b)

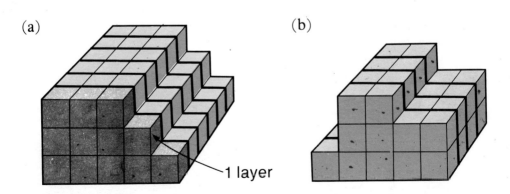

1 layer

Some of these models are built in layers upwards.
Some are built with layers side by side.

For each building, write down

(a) the number of cubes in one layer

(b) the number of layers

(c) the volume of the model, in cubic cm

B3

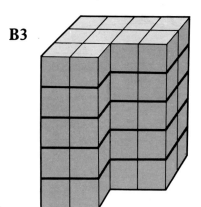

B4

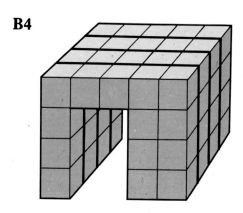

B5

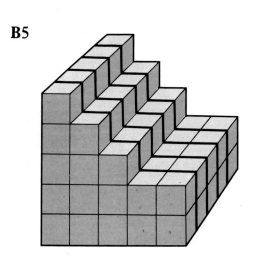

B6

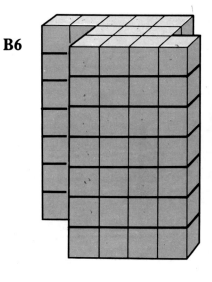

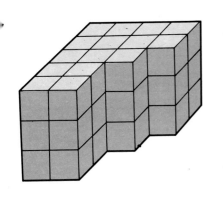

B8

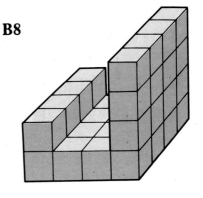

9

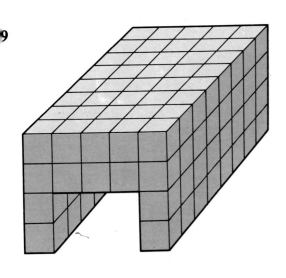

B10

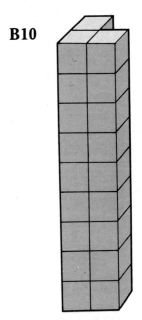

11

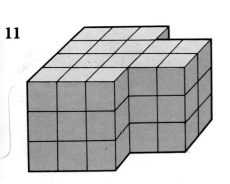

B12

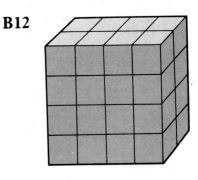

C Prisms

A model which can be split into layers
which are all exactly the same
is called a **prism**.

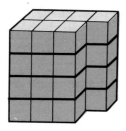  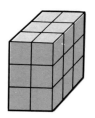

Prisms

Now look at this model.

It can be built in layers upwards,
but the layers are **not** all the same.
They get smaller towards the top.

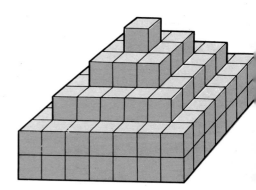

If it is built in side-by-side
layers, these layers are not
all the same either.

So this model is **not** a prism.

C1 Which of these models are prisms?
Write 'yes' or 'no' for each one.

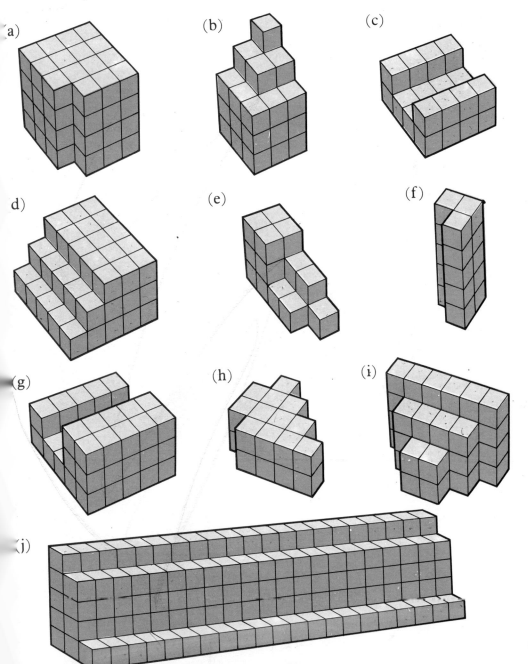

(a)

(b)

(c)

(d)

(e)

(f)

(g)

(h)

(i)

(j)

61

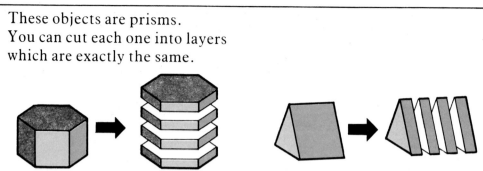

These objects are prisms.
You can cut each one into layers
which are exactly the same.

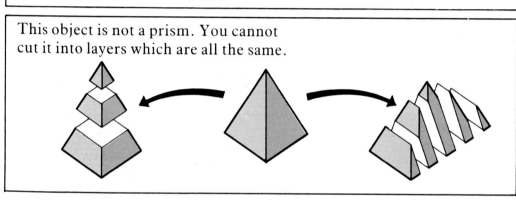

This object is not a prism. You cannot
cut it into layers which are all the same.

C2 Some of these objects are prisms, and some are not.
Draw the ones which are prisms.
Show them split up into layers, like this 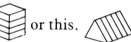 or this.

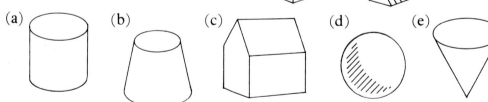

(a)   (b)   (c)   (d)   (e)

C3 Which of these are prisms?

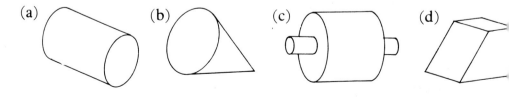

(a)   (b)   (c)   (d)

62

Here is a prism being cut into layers, or slices.	The shape of each slice where the knife cuts it is the same all through.

It is called the **cross-section** of the prism.

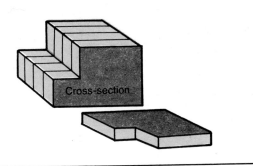

Cross-section

C4 (a) What is the area of the cross-section of this prism, in sq cm?

(b) What is the volume of each layer, in cubic cm?

(c) What is the volume of the prism?

C5

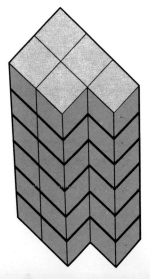

(a) What is the area of the cross-section of this prism?

(b) What is the volume of each layer?

(c) What is the volume of the prism?

63

D Calculating the volume of a prism

The area of the cross-section of this prism is 7 sq cm.

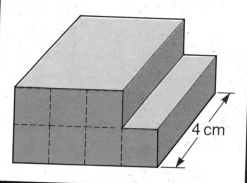

4 cm

So each layer 1 cm thick contains 7 cubic cm.

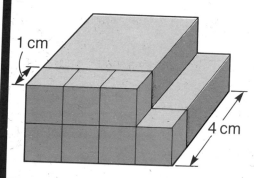

1 cm

4 cm

The prism is 4 cm long, so there are 4 layers.

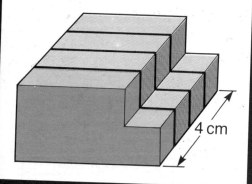

4 cm

So the volume of the prism is 7 × 4 cubic cm = 28 cubic cm.

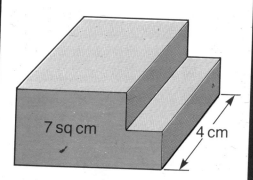

7 sq cm

4 cm

To work out the volume of a prism multiply the area of its cross-section by its length.

1 Work out the volumes of these prisms.

(a)

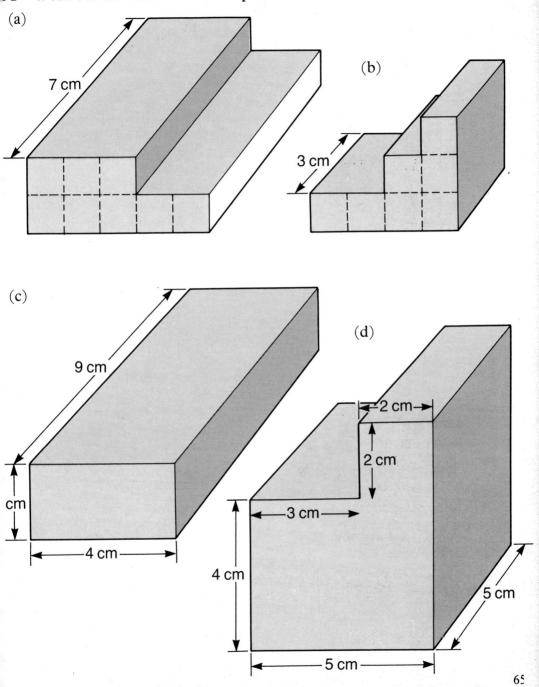

7 cm

(b)

3 cm

(c)

9 cm

cm

4 cm

(d)

2 cm

2 cm

3 cm

4 cm

5 cm

5 cm

D2 Work out the volumes of these prisms.
All measurements are in centimetres.

(a)

(b)

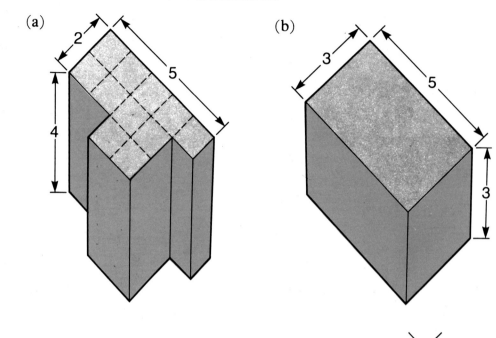

D3 (a) What is the volume of the hole in this prism?
(Measurements are in centimetres.)

(b) What would the volume of the prism be if the hole were filled in?

(c) What is the volume of the prism?

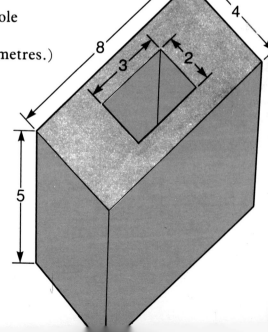

E Volumes of liquids

When you are measuring the volume of a liquid,
1 cubic cm is called **1 millilitre** (1 ml).

A medicine spoon holds 5 ml.

1000 ml make **1 litre.**
So 1 litre is the same as 1000 cubic cm.

A plastic cube 10 cm by 10 cm by 10 cm
has a volume of 1000 cubic cm.
If it is hollow it will hold 1 litre.

E1 An ordinary teacup holds about 200 ml.
Roughly how many medicine spoonfuls does it hold?

E2 How many cups of orange juice can you fill
from a 1 litre carton?

E3 1 ml of water weighs 1 gram.

(a) How many grams does 1 litre of water weigh?

(b) What name do we give to this number of grams?

6 Speed

A Homing pigeons

Six pigeons were released in Coventry at 12 noon.
They arrived home at the times shown on the map.
The map also shows how far they flew.

A1 The Hull pigeon and the Ipswich pigeon
both arrived home at 3 p.m.
Which of them flew faster?

A2 The Luton pigeon arrived home before the Hull pigeon.
▲ Did the Luton pigeon fly faster than the Hull pigeon?

A3 Which was the fastest of the six pigeons?

A4 Which was the slowest?

A5 Make a list of the pigeons in order of their speeds,
fastest first.

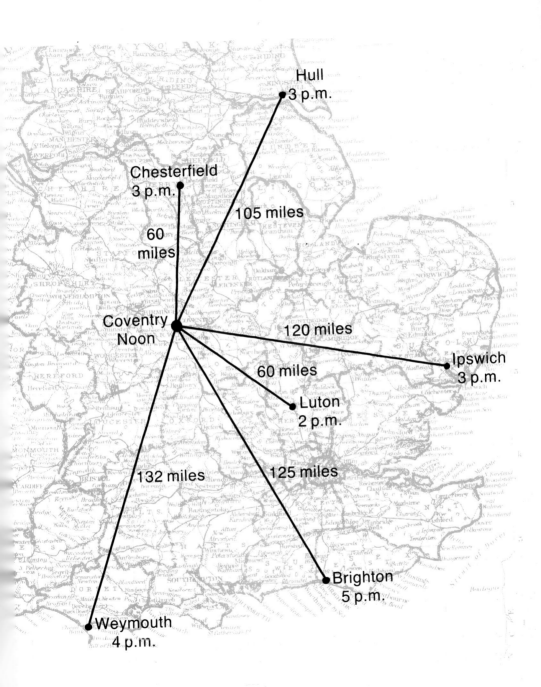

Hull
3 p.m.

Chesterfield
3 p.m.

105 miles

60
miles

Coventry
Noon

120 miles

Ipswich
3 p.m.

60 miles

Luton
2 p.m.

132 miles

125 miles

Brighton
5 p.m.

Weymouth
4 p.m.

B Cars

B1 Picture B was taken 1 second after picture A.

Which car is going faster, the red or the black?

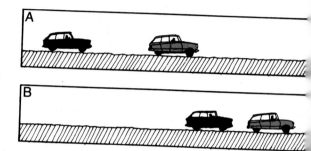

B2 In each pair of pictures below, picture B was taken 1 second after picture A.

Which car is going faster in each case?

(a)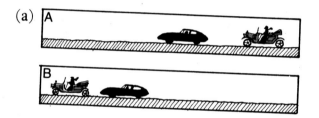

(b)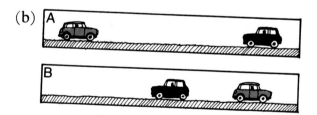

(c)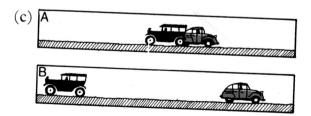

A cycle race

C1 In this picture you are looking down on a cycle race track. Alan (A), Baljit (B) and Colin (C) are just starting a race.

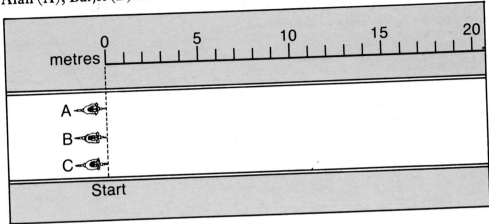

The next picture was taken 1 second later.

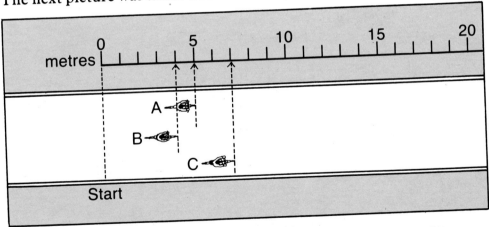

(a) How far did Alan go in 1 second?

(b) How far did Baljit go in 1 second?

(c) How far did Colin go in 1 second?

Alan went 5 metres in 1 second.
We say his **speed** for the first second
of the race was **5 metres per second.**

We write it **5 m/s.**

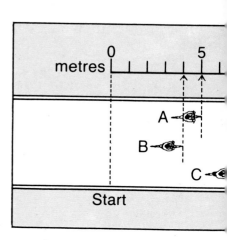

C2 (a) Write down Baljit's speed for
the first second.
(Remember to write m/s.)
(b) Write down Colin's speed.
(c) Who was the fastest starter?

C3 This picture shows the three boys later in the race.

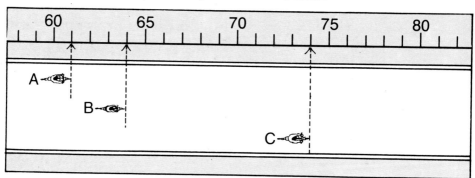

This picture was taken 1 second later.

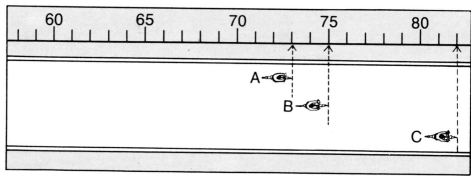

(a) How far did Alan go in that 1 second? (**Not** 73 m!)
(b) Write down Alan's speed for that second.

4 (a) How far did Baljit go in that 1 second?

  (b) Write down Baljit's speed.

  (c) Write down Colin's speed.

5 Whose speed was greatest during that 1 second?

6 This picture was taken near the end of the race.

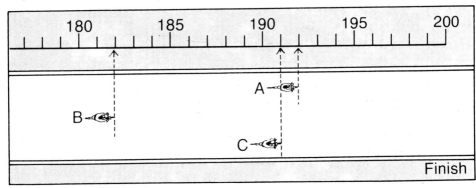

And this was taken 1 second later.

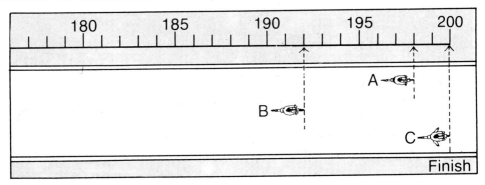

  (a) What was Alan's speed in that second?
  (b) What was Baljit's speed?
  (c) What was Colin's speed?
  (d) Who was slowest in that second?
  (e) Who was fastest?

D Constant speeds

It is very difficult to ride a bike at one steady speed
on ordinary roads.

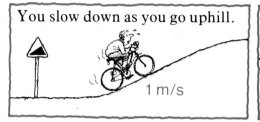

You slow down as you go uphill.

1 m/s

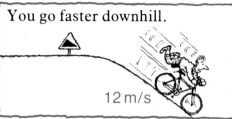

You go faster downhill.

12 m/s

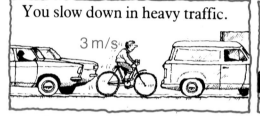

You slow down in heavy traffic.

3 m/s

Sometimes you have to stop.

0 m/s

But on a straight, flat, clear road
you can go at a steady, or **constant**, speed.

7 m/s

If you go at a **constant** speed, you go the same distance
in every second.

If you have a constant speed of 7 m/s, you go 7 m
in every second.

D1 How far do you go in 3 seconds at a constant
speed of 7 m/s?

D2 If you go at a constant speed of 4 m/s, how far
▲   do you go in   (a) 3 seconds   (b) 5 seconds   (c) 10 seconds

74

D3 An express train is going
at a constant speed of 60 m/s.
How far does it go in 8 seconds?

D4 A jet plane is flying at a constant speed of 250 m/s.
How far does it go in 3 seconds?

D5 A cyclist goes uphill at 2 m/s for 7 seconds,
then downhill at 8 m/s for 3 seconds.

How far does he go altogether in that time?

D6

Katy

Bob

Bob is running at a steady speed of 4 m/s.
He overtakes Katy, who is walking
at a steady speed of 1 m/s.

Here they are 5 seconds later.

(a) How far did Bob go in the 5 seconds?

(b) How far did Katy go?

(c) How far apart were they after the 5 seconds?

(d) How far apart will they be after another 5 seconds?

 A game for two players

You need a dice, and two markers like these.

Read the instructions right through first.

1 Put your markers at 0.

2 You take turns to say how many seconds each round should be. It can be 1, 2, 3, 4 or 5.

3 When the number of seconds has been chosen for the round, you each throw the dice once.

This table shows your speed for that round.

For example, suppose player 1 decides the round should be **3 seconds.**

Player 1 throws a ⚅ . So he goes at 6 m/s for 3 seconds. That is 18 m. So he moves his marker along 18 m.

Player 2 throws a ⚂ . So he goes at 3 m/s for 3 seconds. That is 9 m. So he moves his marker along 9 m.

4 The first to cross the finishing line is the winner.

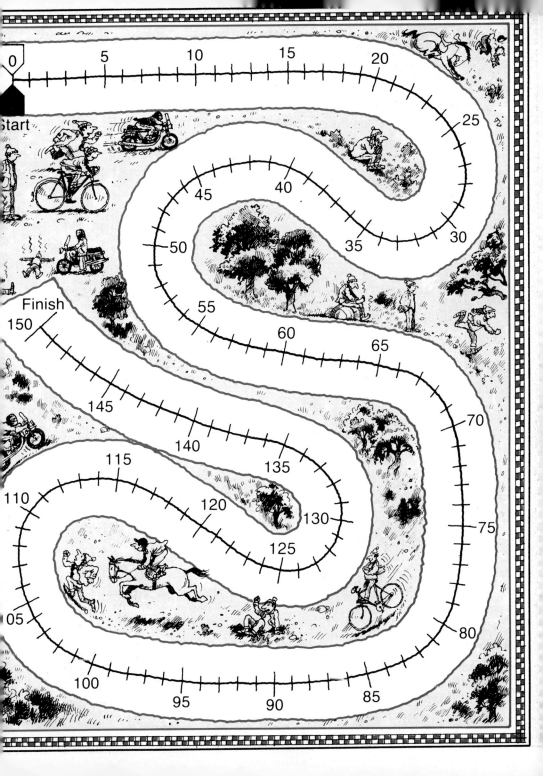

E Distance-time graphs

Tony is a long-distance walker.
He goes at a constant speed of 4 m/s.

Here are some pictures of him at the start of a walk.

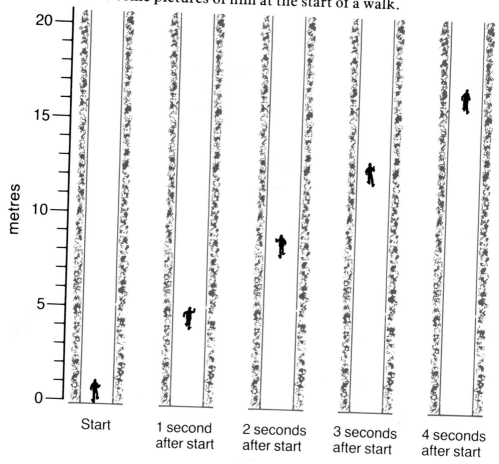

E1 (a) How far has Tony walked 3 seconds after the start?

(b) How far has he walked 5 seconds after the start?

(c) How far has he walked $1\frac{1}{2}$ seconds after the start?

Instead of pictures we can draw a graph like this.
It is called a **distance-time graph**.

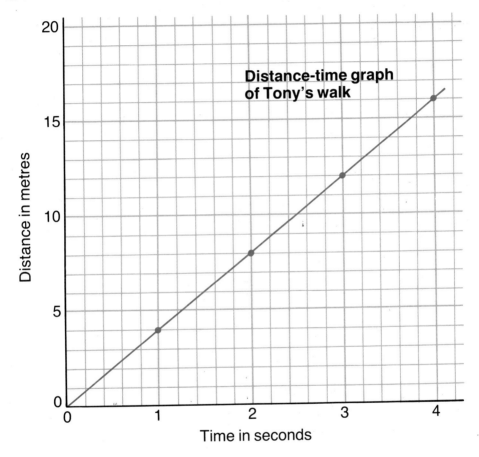

Distance-time graph of Tony's walk

2 Use the graph to answer these questions.

(a) How far has Tony gone after 0·5 seconds?

(b) How far has he gone after 3·5 seconds?

(c) How long does it take him to walk 10 metres?

Gertie is another walker.
She and Tony start at the same time.

Here are their distance-time graphs.

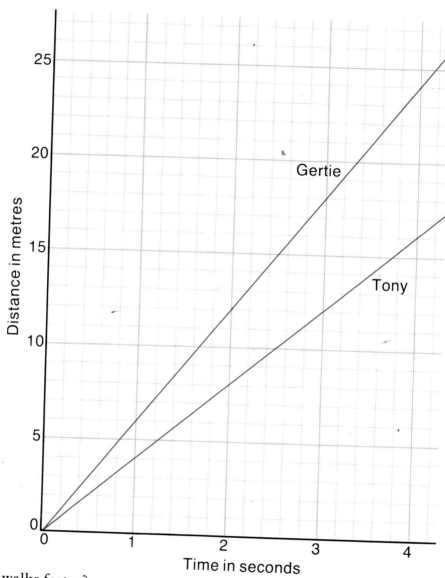

E3 Who walks faster?

4 (a) How far has Gertie gone after 1 second?

    (b) How far has she gone after 2 seconds?

    (c) Does she go the same distance in every second?

    (d) What is her speed in m/s?

5 (a) How far has Gertie gone after 4 seconds?

    (b) How far ahead of Tony is she then?

6 A runner and a cyclist start together.
The runner goes at 5 m/s.
The cyclist goes at 8 m/s.

    (a) Copy and complete these tables.

Runner

Time in seconds	0	1	2	3	4	5
Distance in metres	0	5				

Cyclist

Time in seconds	0	1	2	3	4	5
Distance in metres	0					

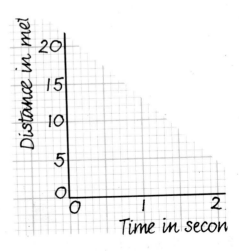

    (b) Draw axes on graph paper. ⇨
Make sure they are long enough
for the numbers in both tables.

        Draw both distance–time graphs
on the same axes
(like those on the opposite page).

    (c) How far apart are the
cyclist and the runner
3·5 seconds from the start?

    (d) There is a tree 20 m from the start.
When does the cyclist pass it?

    (e) When does the runner pass it?

E7 Here are the distance-time graphs
of three cyclists, A, B and C.

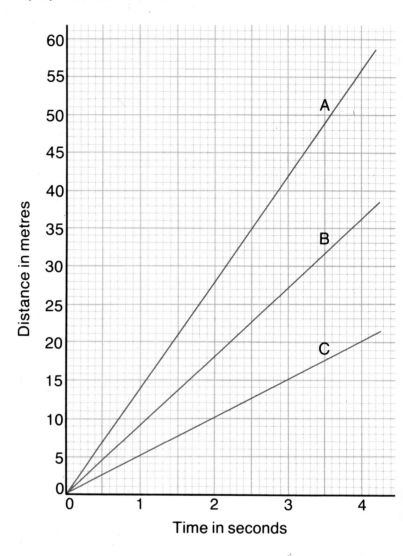

(a) Which cyclist is fastest?   (b) Which is slowest?

(c) How far did A go in 1 second?   (d) What is A's speed?

(e) What is B's speed?   (f) What is C's speed?

8 This graph shows a race between two old cars.

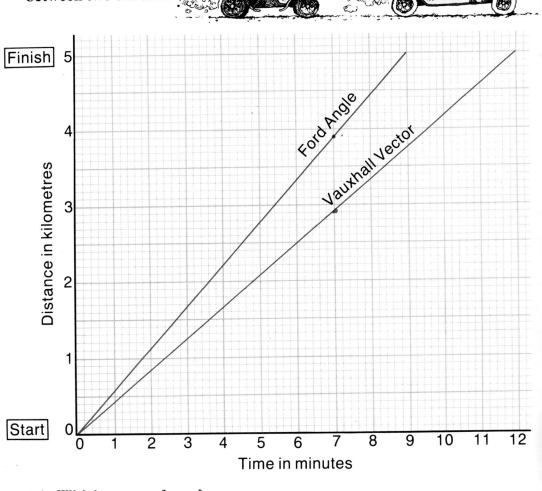

(a) Which car was faster?

(b) How many minutes did the winner take to finish?

(c) How many minutes were there between the winner finishing and the loser finishing?

(d) How far did the Vauxhall Vector go in 7 minutes?

(e) How far ahead was the Ford Angle after 7 minutes?

F   Changing speed

Up to now every graph has shown a constant speed.
In the next question there is a change in speed.

F1 A man walks at 5 m/s for 4 seconds.
Then he changes to 2 m/s and goes for 3 seconds.

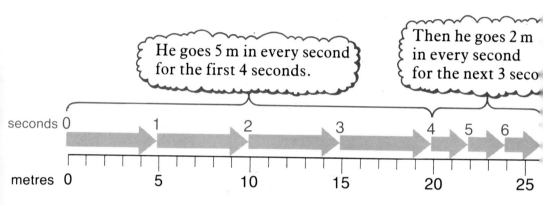

He goes 5 m in every second for the first 4 seconds.

Then he goes 2 m in every second for the next 3 seco

(a) Copy and complete this table.

Time in seconds	0	1	2	3	4	5	6	7
Distance in metres								

(b) Draw axes on graph paper.

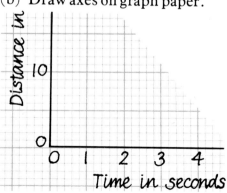

(c) Draw the graph.
It will look something
like this.

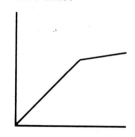

2 A girl walks for 3 seconds at 4 m/s
and then runs for 5 seconds at 9 m/s.

(a) Copy and complete this table.

Time in seconds	0	1	2	3	4	5	6	7	8
Distance in metres	0	4			21				

(b) Draw the distance-time graph.

F3 Here are the distance-time
graphs of three cyclists.

(a) Which cyclist went slowly
at first, then speeded up?

(b) Which one went fast
at first, then slowed down?

(c) Which one went at
a constant speed?

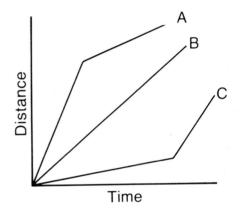

4 This is the distance-time graph of a runner.

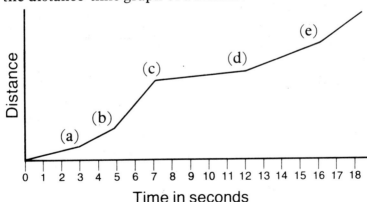

What did he do at each of these times?
Did he speed up or did he slow down?

(a) 3 sec   (b) 5 sec   (c) 7 sec   (d) 12 sec   (e) 16 sec

7 Views

On the platform at Slough station
there is a stuffed dog in a glass case.
The dog's name is Jim.

When Jim was alive, he collected money for
charity. Every time someone dropped a coin
into one of his collecting bags, he barked.

Jim died in 1896.

This is what you see when you look
at Jim from the front.
This picture is called a **front view** of Jim.

This is what you see when you look
at Jim from the side.
This is a **side view** of Jim.

This is what you see when you look at Jim from above.
This is a **top view** or **plan view** of Jim.

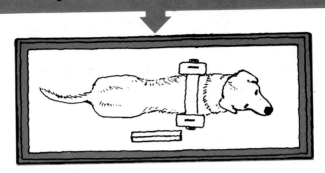

This artist is drawing a **back view** of Jim.

Does he draw Jim's head
pointing to the **left,**   or the **right?**

A2 Frod Cars are showing three new models at the Motor Show.

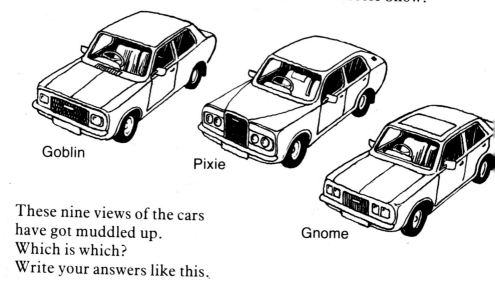

Goblin

Pixie

Gnome

These nine views of the cars
have got muddled up.
Which is which?
Write your answers like this.

(a) is a side view of the Pixie   and so on.

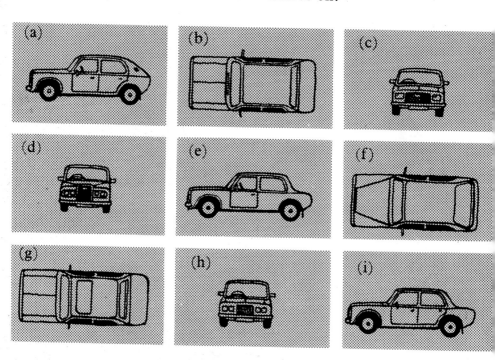

B Views of a model house

You need worksheet BT-4, scissors, glue.

1 Cut out the model.
Fold carefully along the dotted lines.

2 If you want to colour your model house,
colour it before you stick it together.

3 Stick the chimney together first, like this.

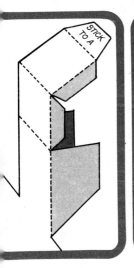
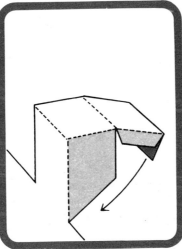

4 Stick the rest of
the model together.

Stick the chimney
to the roof at A.

Stand your model on the rectangle below.
Make sure the front door is in the right place.
(The front door has a letter box.)

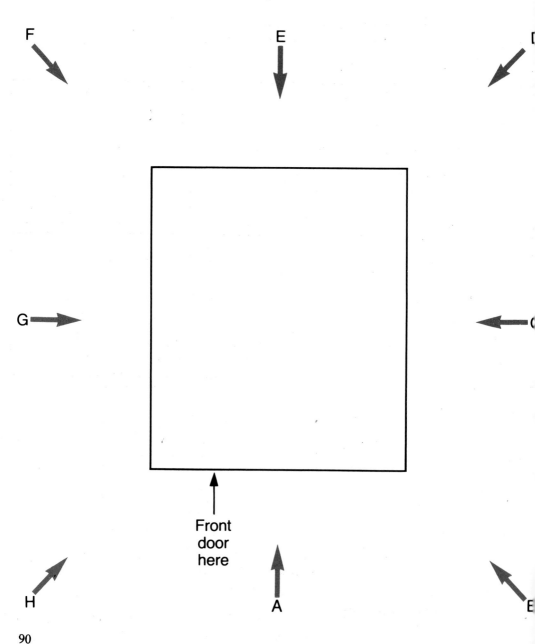

F

E

D

G

C

Front
door
here

H

A

B

B1 Here are 8 views of the house.
Each view shows what you see when you look
in the direction of one of the arrows A to H.

Which arrow goes with each view?
**Try to do this question first without looking
round the model.**

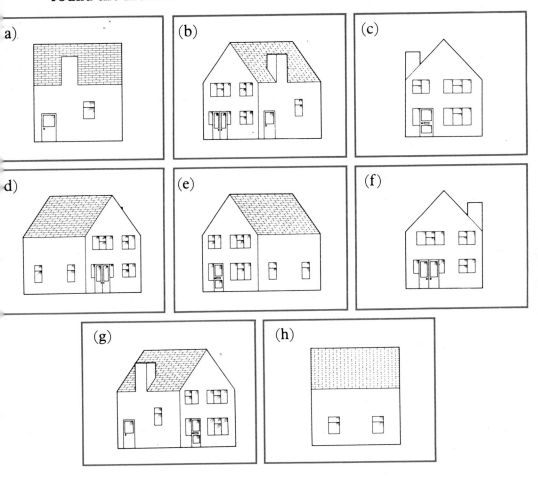

a)

(b)

(c)

d)

(e)

(f)

(g)

(h)

B2 Draw a **top view** (or **plan view**) of the house.
It is what you see when you look down on it
from directly overhead.

C Buildings

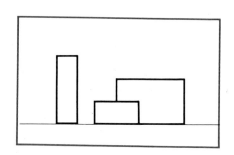

You need 3 ordinary size matchboxes
                worksheet BT-5.

This is an architect's model
of a new town centre.
There is a plan of the town centre
on the worksheet.

Stand the 3 matchboxes on the 3 rectangles
on the plan.
Now you have a simple model of the town centre.

C1 This is a view of the town centre
▲   from the west.

What direction do you look from
to see each of these views?

(a)
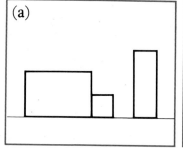

(b)
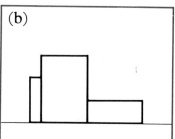

(c)
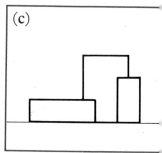

2 This is a model of a new school.

There is a plan of the school
on the worksheet.
Stand the 3 matchboxes
on the plan.

What direction do you look from
to see each of these views?

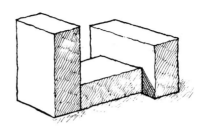

(a)

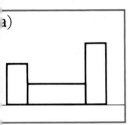

(b)

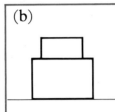

(c)

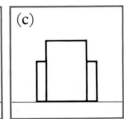

(d)

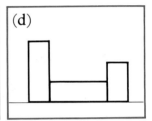

3 This is a model of a hospital.

Stand the 3 matchboxes
on the plan of the hospital.
What direction do you look from
to see each of these views?

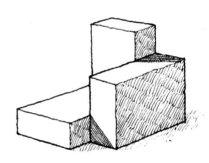

(a)

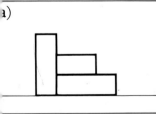

(b)

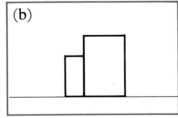

(c)

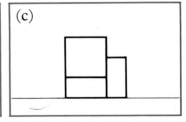

(d)

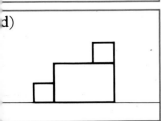

(e)

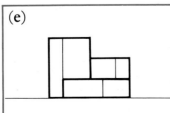

(f)

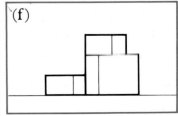

Put the worksheet back.
You will not need it any more.

C4 Make this model building with 2 matchboxes.
▲

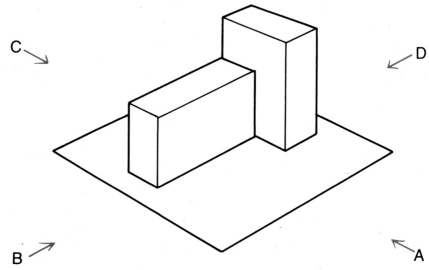

Draw 4 views of the model, from directions A, B, C, D.

Letter your drawings A, B, C, D.

C5 Draw a **top view** of the model in question C4.

C6 Make this model and
draw 4 views of it.

Letter your views
A, B, C, D.

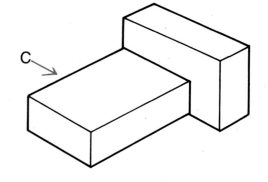

C7 Draw a top view of the model in question C6.

Puzzles

Who sees each of these views of the tea-set?

(a)

(b)

(c)

(d)

D2 Here are some views of well-known objects.
Can you name the objects?
There are two views of each object.

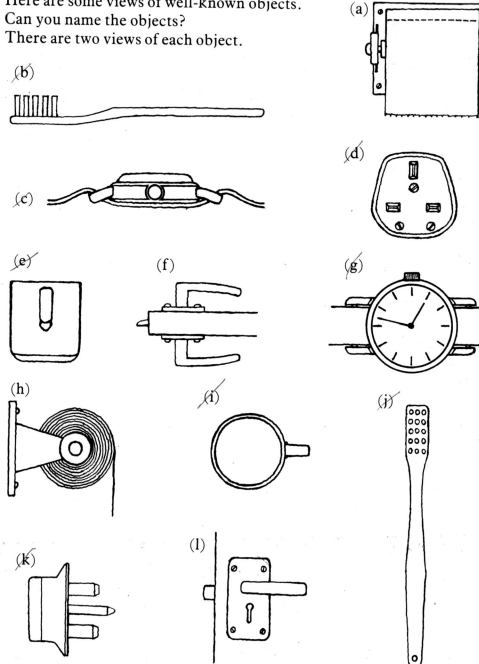

(a)

(b)

(c)

(d)

(e)

(f)

(g)

(h)

(i)

(j)

(k)

(l)